The Writer's Eye

William Dalrymple

The Writer's Eye

William Dalrymple

Introduction by
Siddharth Dhanvant Shanghvi

Introduction

At a dinner in Goa, in the winter of 2014, William Dalrymple pulled out his phone and showed me some photographs from his travels. This was a noisy party, guests were chatting animatedly, wine glasses were being refilled. But even in the elegant disquiet of the evening, the photographs held their own. They exuded a solid quietness; I recognized something clean and powerful, a kiln fire. Like thread sliding through a needle's eye, my attention passed into the photographs. Later, I felt that encountering the photographs at the dinner party was akin to seeing a sage in a bazaar: life was the same noisy, mostly pointless thing for everyone, but accidental sacredness was everywhere, too. I wrote to William, requesting if I might see other pictures. I told him that I was very interested that the photographs had been made on a phone; I increasingly believe some part of serious photographic future will be made on the phone; the medium offers lightening immediacy and, when used sensitively, encourages an intimacy that sometimes comes in the way of the camera as an object. Already, change is at hand. Sooni Taraporevala, for instance, shot a handsome photo essay entirely on her iPhone; Ai Weiwei has a flourishing Instagram account.

A year passed; we resumed the conversation; there were more pictures to look at.

It might be easy to think of the pictures as being about place – mountains with peculiar grooves hinting to abandoned civilization; deserted beaches where light strains through sea mist; an artist's studio, with half completed models; great boulders seething against the horizon. But perhaps that's me being lazy. The more time I spent with the photographs, the more I felt what had drawn me to them was the same quality that attracted me to the novels of Virginia Woolf: their interiority. It might be simple enough to say Woolf's novels are about the 'stream of consciousness' or certain important themes like gender and sexuality – of course they are. But more acutely, the books are about where the act of serious reading can bring you, beyond intellectual shimmer and bounce, to pause and revelation. Great books carry seeds of solitude, they take in your quiet and give you their own: in the parenthesis of this shared exchange we may reassess, examine, splinter, mend, and persist.

Sometimes photographs also have this quality, they no longer serve as visual proof of what exists but become intimations of what is unknown, and only deeply felt.

Rilke, writing about music, called it 'the breathing of statues'. He recognized that music was a portal; in the act of listening one could enter another realm, one could, as Sufi art has shown over centuries, transcend the unknown world in order to know it, and perhaps become some part of it. While the photographs in this suite document expanses and vistas, they are equally about the retreat and cowering one makes in oneself only to unexpectedly find nameless, deserted, sometimes beautiful precincts. This is why naming the places, trying to locate where each photograph was made, providing them provenance or date, may only diminish where Dalrymple's pictures can lead you. The more I looked at the images, the more indistinct I felt; my most private isolation was writ large in his depiction of an abandoned shoreline, in foreboding cloud shadow, in theatrical, perpendicular shots of harvested fields.

The photographs took me back to the same dangerous place good writing dares me to enter, a chamber of questioning.

Have other writers attempted photography? Certainly, and most recently, Teju Cole, whose essays on the subject have been influential. What might a writer bring to the medium? Two decades of his practice as a writer – feted, beloved and justly appreciated for subject as well as style – Dalrymple comes to the ground with economy, composition and muscular elegance for a craft that he first practiced as a student and returns to being a disciple of language. What the pictures withhold is equally telling of them, as they are of how restraint is a good writer's forte. In one of the most striking photographs here, you wonder why the dog lopes across the shore: is he out on a friendly run, perhaps playing fetch? Or is he running from something the photographer leaves for us to decode, pumping into an otherwise beautiful photograph eerie narrative tension?

The bookmaker, Dayanita Singh, has frequently referenced the influence of literature on her photographs; these are mostly aesthetic, emotional, or psychological shadows. In Dalrymple's case the photographs carry the technical precision of a writer constantly economizing, burning down his sentence to its essence. While the photographs are panoramic, sweeping, full of range, the net cast wide catches the singular telling detail that evidences how the image is beholden to language and its measure. You see it in the images of the boulder, which might be easily lost, but all of a sudden you see a spool, which then repeats in the sky, in the cloud, in the shadow it casts; inadvertently, they become formalist statements, tracking pattern and repetition that may or may not be coincidental. Unlike the non-fiction accounts in his books, these photographs don't offer explanation: they don't need to, being whole unto themselves, as more than literal representation, as tiny, perfect mirrors of longing and contemplation. But while the books are distinguished by their historical sweep and exactitude, the photographs have the quality of a lake, a great bowl containing life and death, a flickering of the ineffable. This makes photography a fresh, even exciting, language for his exploration.

The pictures are also about an early place in an artist's life, perhaps the same room where the writing lived before it was made into book. Such places are temples where you don't know the name of the God, but you know you are in the presence of something divine. Once things are named and known, admired and adored, something essential leaves them; they become communal things. These photographs may soon become public documents, but right now they are humming with mystery and doubt, the swan right before its flight.

Siddharth Dhanvant Shanghvi

The Writer's Eye

In the gusty, blustery, leaf-blown autumn of 1986, the painter, Derek Hill, rang out of the blue and invited me to lunch at his club in St James's. He was then about seventy; I was twenty-one. The reason for the sudden invitation soon became clear. I was just back from a journey following in the footsteps of Marco Polo, and Derek wanted me to bring to the lunch some of the Mongol roof tiles I had found at Polo's final destination, Kubla Khan's summer palace at Xanadu. The lunch, he explained, was for a friend of his who particularly wanted to see them.

That friend turned out to be the travel writer, Bruce Chatwin, and the lunch was one of those rare encounters that happen only once or twice in a lifetime and really do change your entire trajectory. Chatwin, I thought, was simply astounding. As we sat in the hush of the panelled dining room, surrounded by whispering pin-striped clubmen, my small fragments of glazed tile were the starting point for a conversational riff that moved from the nomads of Mongolia in the thirteenth century and cantered over the steppes to Timurid Herat, then leapt polymathically to Ibn Battuta, Ibn Khaldun, Sufi sheikhs and the shamans of the Kalahari bushmen; before long we were being told about Taoist sages, aboriginal 'dreaming' pictures and ancient Cycladic sculpture and hence, as coffee came, via Proust and Pascal and Berenson, to Derek's portraits, and the latter's story about sharing a railway carriage with Robert Byron who performed a pitch-perfect imitation of Queen Victoria using the train's antimacassar as the Queen's mourning veil.

At the end, Chatwin limped off on crutches to the London Library saying he needed to check some references for his forthcoming book on the aborigines of Central Australia: though it had not been apparent while seated at the lunch, he was already very weak from the AIDS that would eventually kill him. After he had gone, I wandered through the park in the bright autumn sunlight, rabbit-in-the-headlights dazzled by the whole performance: I'd never come across anyone like him, or met anyone who even approached him as a conversationalist. I'm not sure I ever have since.

A couple of years later, after Chatwin's death, aged only 48, it emerged that he was also a remarkable photographer, and the brilliant collection of his images that were published after his death – images that ranged from the Sahara to the Pacific, from Afghanistan to Mount Athos – were full of surprises, even to those who thought they knew him well. It was also an object lesson as to what happens when a writer takes photographs.

For sometimes, with luck, a photograph can reveal a quite different side to a writer's character and vision to the one revealed in their texts. Chatwin was a writer of breathtaking prose – prose whose crystal-cool clarity and bleak, chiselled beauty, as startling as a Verey light, and as precise as a surgeon's knife, was worked and reworked, polished and polished again, as he patiently cut his sentences down to their essence. Yet Chatwin's photography was far more immediate and feline than his writing: his best images are those that capture the fleeting moment. They were grabbed on the hoof, on his Leica, often without forethought or planning, and the best of them have the sudden, instant perfection of a cat's flawless all-four-paws landing. His images also have a wonderfully reciprocal relationship with the modernist painters that he loved: the tin shacks of Mali turned in an instant into beautiful formalist compositions, squares of pure colour with echoes of Léger and Kandinsky.

It is of course difficult – and maybe even dangerous – for any artist to analyse his own work, but looking now at these images of mine culled from the last eighteen months of travels from Leh to Lindisfarne, from the Hindu Kush to the Lammermuirs and across the rolling hills south of Sienna, I think they also show a rather different palette to that visible in my writing. Certainly they have been inspired by the same travels and there are common themes – Mughal architecture, the ruins of Afghanistan, the domes of Golconda – but the photographs show, I think, a taste for the dark and remote, the moody and the atmospheric, perhaps even the Gothic, that I don't think is there in my books or articles and which slightly surprises even me.

If I was to look for a source, I suspect they draw deeply on the images that impregnated my Scottish childhood and youth. I was brought up on the cold and wind-swept shores of the Firth of Forth, looking out over the breakers of the North Sea, and educated at a curious monastic school in the wild, bleak sheep-tracts of the Yorkshire Moors. My first eighteen years were spent far from any metropolis, under dark northern skies, right on the edge of things. The remote places celebrated in these photographs reflect, I think, a taste for the austere, ascetic and windswept forms of those years.

Photography for me long preceded writing. In fact, it is in my blood. My Calcutta-born, part-Bengali great-great-aunt was Julia Margaret Cameron, one of the greatest photographers of the nineteenth century. A force of nature, she would waylay anyone and rarely took no for an answer, taking shots of them to illustrate Tennyson's *Idylls of the King*. Victorian politicians such as Gladstone and Disraeli, as well as Tennyson, Darwin and Watts, would be draped in rugs and tinsel crowns and made to pose as King Arthur, while their wives, servant girls and even stray passers-by, willing and unwilling, would be dressed up as Queen Guinevere or the Lady of the Lake. As a child in Scotland, I used to leaf through her portraits in the albums we had at home and envy the world she had created and her ability to make such luminous, telling and painterly portraits with a camera.

I have taken photographs since I was first given a tiny Kodak for my seventh birthday, but when I was fifteen I was left some money by a relation and spent it on a fabulous Contax 35mm SLR with a pin-sharp Carl Zeiss T* lens. For the next five years I spent much of my time in the school dark room, emerging after several hours stinking of fixer, with water-logged hands, and developer splashed all over my clothes, but clutching a precious sheaf of 10x8 prints.

I always preferred black and white, partly because it allowed me to develop and edit my own prints; but mainly because black and white seemed a much more daring and exciting world, full of artistic possibilities. 'Black,' wrote Matisse – a man who knew something about colour – 'is a force,' and I have always believed that black and white has a visceral power that colour can never match.

As a teenager, I spent a lot of time leafing through photographic books and particularly admired the bleak and grainy war photography of Don McCullin and the landscape work of Fay Godwin. But my real hero was Bill Brandt, whose darkly brooding images were marked by a stark chiaroscuro, a strongly geometrical sense of composition, a whiff of the surreal and a taste for the uncanny and unsettling.

'It is part of the photographer's job to see more intensely than most people do,' he wrote. 'He must have and keep in him something of the receptiveness of the child who looks at the world for the first time, or the traveller who enters a strange country. Most photographers would feel a sense of embarrassment in admitting publicly that they carried within them a sense of wonder, yet without it they would not produce the work they do. It is the gift of seeing the light around them clearly and vividly, as something that is exciting in its own right.' I have made this my mantra as a photographer.

Inspired by Brandt, I always tried to push my prints to make them as gritty as possible, and used to prefer grainy HP5 film and high contrast papers. Dodging and cropping, burning and using collage, I attempted to mirror Brandt's anthracite skies and velvety jet-black landscapes, trying to capture the same bleakness that he was able to read into the hills and towns he captured on film. In time, I won a couple of regional, and then national, young photographer awards.

At Cambridge, it was penning a review of a Fay Godwin show for the student paper that first led me into journalism and writing. During my college days, I spent as much, if not more, time shooting and developing photographs as I did typing out pieces. When I went on my long-haul journey in the footsteps of Marco Polo, the subject of my first book *In Xanadu*, I took as much care with the photographs as I did with my notes, and the book is filled with my black-and-white shots from the journey. This became the material of my first large-scale photographic exhibition, *Hajj: An Islamic Pilgrimage*, in 1986.

In time, however, writing took over from photography as my artistic outlet, and my precious Contax came to languish unused in its bag in a cupboard. It is only in the last eighteen months, since I jettisoned my last Blackberry for a Samsung Note, that I have rediscovered my passion for photography. I now have an excellent little camera tucked away permanently in my back pocket. Discovering Snapseed edit suite last winter has allowed me to produce the sort of grainy black-and-white images I love best for the first time in twenty-five years. And these days, advances in technology mean that I can produce this work without covering myself with chemicals.

The primary inspiration has been my travels, and this collection is a record of a restless year, between books, when I took the opportunity to visit some of the world's most remote places, especially in Central Asia. I'll never forget the astonishing flight last year over the rib-cage of the Hindu Kush to Bamiyan, the dark slopes all etched in ice, each river valley white against the black granite of range after range of folding mountains. In the centre of the Pamirs, on the roof of the world mid-way from Kabul to Bamiyan, there are no signs of any habitation: it is a clear, empty, silent landscape lined with frozen crevice-skeletons of unmelted snow. In many ways it feels a primeval landscape, as untouched by man as it was when the lava had first flowed from volcanoes.

Bamiyan means The Place of Shining Light, and there is indeed something quite out-of-the-ordinary about the clarity and sharp intensity of the light illuminating this hidden valley, hanging suspended in the Hindu Kush. As we touched down on the high-altitude airstrip, the lines of poplars all around us were turning a molten autumnal yellow against the pale salmon-pink of the cliffs. Here, even at a distance, the bright, slanting morning light picked out with great precision the strangely moving vision of the two vast empty niches. There is a real and significant presence here still, even in the absence of the figures they once contained.

Other fruitful sources of images have been treks through the stupa fields and mani walls of Ladakh; visits to Yazd, Pasargadae and the deserts of western Iran; a journey along the Ganges looking for ittar in Kannauj; the marshes and causeways of coastal Northumbria; even the bizarre Kandinsky-like irrigation works in the desert fringes of Idaho. The chaos of the chowks of Lucknow and the crumbling Paigah palaces of old Hyderabad were also fruitful hunting grounds, as were summer walks through the olive hills of Tuscany and the bleak but beloved beaches of my Scottish childhood, with their extraordinary rock strata and violent geomorphology.

Through all these travels, I carried my humble Samsung cellphone. I get a particular pleasure out of the immediacy and the lack of pretension inherent in using a cellphone to record the world around me. For photography should always be about the eye, not the equipment. Brandt believed this strongly: 'Photography is still a very new medium and everything must be tried and dared,' he wrote. 'Photography has no rules. It is not a sport. It is the result that counts, no matter how it is achieved…. No amount of toying with shades of print or with printing papers will transform a commonplace photograph into anything other than a commonplace photograph.' It is, in other words, the vision that counts, not the camera.

Just as black and white has a greater intensity than colour, breaking down reality into an essence and emphasising pattern and signal over noise, so using so simple an instrument as a cellphone raises vision over technique: you are not distracted by light meters, you don't have to stop to consider depth of field; composition is all. You try to capture the moment, to see patterns in a landscape, tell stories in chance encounters, and create a measure of order out of random chaos. You try to stop for one millisecond the relentless trajectory of Time's Arrow. Moreover, if the image is a success, no one can attribute it to fancy equipment.

For me Brandt remains the master and looking afresh at these images while writing this piece, I am astonished to see the unconscious influence he still has on my photography: so many of the shots I produce now, aged fifty, are clearly influenced by work of his I last saw in my early twenties – a testament, perhaps, to the degree to which great images are capable of lodging themselves in our unconscious and influencing the way we see, even many years later.

William Dalrymple

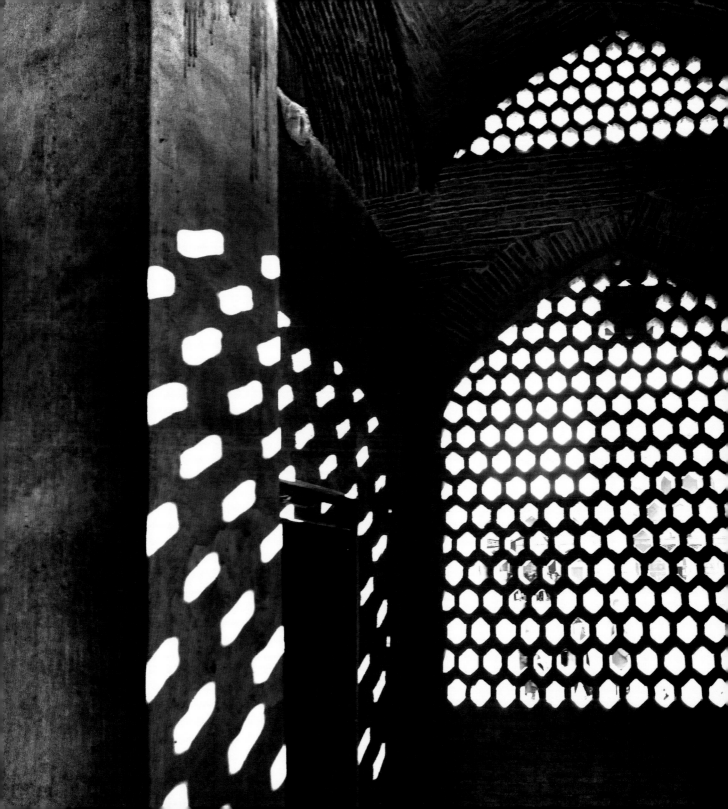

Acknowledgements

Dattaraj and Dipti Salgaocar, Isheta Salgaocar,
Roshini Vadehra, Conor Macklin, David Godwin,
Ananth, Somak Ghoshal, Bonita Vaz-Shimray,
Nilima Menezes, Devika Daulet-Singh.

Special thanks
Abhinav Anguria, Anup Patil, Ganesh Mahajan, Siddhanth Sheorey,
Shantanu Sheorey & Vanmayi Shetty, students and faculty
at The One School Goa for their excellent and tireless assistance.

Olivia, Ibby, Sam & Adam Dalrymple.

Sunaparanta Goa Centre for The Arts was founded by Dattaraj and Dipti Salgaocar. It is a not-for-profit, process-based public arts space that dialogues directly and freely with the community to encourage creation, learning, understanding, and appreciation of various art forms. Over the years, Sunaparanta has showed work from nationally and internationally acclaimed artists such as Dayanita Singh, Julian Opie, Vasco Araújo, and hosted lectures by Anne Enright, Roger Ballen, Jitish Kallat and other stalwarts of the artistic world.

William Dalrymple is a writer, traveller and historian as well as a curator, critic and one of the co-directors and founders of the annual Jaipur Literature Festival. He is the author of several bestselling books, including *Return of a King*, *White Mughals* and *Nine Lives*.

Siddharth Dhanvant Shanghvi's debut novel, *The Last Song of Dusk*, won the Betty Trask Award in the UK, the Premio Grinzane Cavour in Italy, and was nominated for the IMPAC Prize. *The Lost Flamingoes of Bombay*, his subsequent bestselling novel, was nominated for the Man Asian Literary Prize 2008.

First published in 2016 by HarperCollins *Publishers* India

Copyright © Sunaparanta 2016
Photographs and essay copyright © William Dalrymple 2016
Introduction copyright © Siddharth Dhanvant Shanghvi 2016

P-ISBN: 9789351779254
E-ISBN: 9789351779261

2 4 6 8 10 9 7 5 3 1

HarperCollins *Publishers*
A-75, Sector 57, Noida, Uttar Pradesh 201301, India
1 London Bridge Street, London SE1 9GF, United Kingdom
Hazelton Lanes, 55 Avenue Road, Suite 2900, Toronto, Ontario M5R 3L2
and 1995 Markham Road, Scarborough, Ontario M1B 5M8, Canada
25 Ryde Road, Pymble, Sydney, NSW 2073, Australia
10 East 53rd Street, New York NY 10022, USA

Typeset in Avenir Lt Std

Printed and bound at Thomson Press (India) Ltd.